CW01260932

# Horse Whispering in the Military Industrial Complex

PHILIP WELLS performs as The Fire Poet everywhere from St Paul's Cathedral to Channings Wood Prison, from Buckingham Palace to children's hospices, from 11 Downing Street to children's psychiatric units, in front of everyone from Robbie Williams to Gordon Brown. He has written an opera about Thomas Becket which was performed in Canterbury Cathedral. He has collaborated with rock bands, photographers, sculptors, painters and fire jugglers. Currently he is making poetry films on Second Life.

# Horse Whispering in the Military Industrial Complex

PHILIP WELLS

PUBLISHED BY SALT PUBLISHING
14a High Street, Fulbourn, Cambridge CB21 5DH United Kingdom

All rights reserved

© Philip Wells, 2009

The right of Philip Wells to be identified as the
author of this work has been asserted by him in accordance
with Section 77 of the Copyright, Designs and Patents Act 1988.

This book is in copyright. Subject to statutory exception
and to provisions of relevant collective licensing agreements,
no reproduction of any part may take place without the written
permission of Salt Publishing.

First published 2009

Printed by the MPG Books Group in the UK

Typeset in Swift 9.5 / 13

*This book is sold subject to the conditions that it shall not,
by way of trade or otherwise, be lent, re-sold, hired out,
or otherwise circulated without the publisher's prior consent
in any form of binding or cover other than that in which
it is published and without a similar condition including this
condition being imposed on the subsequent purchaser.*

ISBN 978 1 84471 479 7 hardback

Salt Publishing Ltd gratefully acknowledges
the financial assistance of Arts Council England

1 3 5 7 9 8 6 4 2

*For Elizabeth*

*Words may be deeds*
—AESOP

# Contents

| | |
|---|---|
| We Have Come | 1 |
| Hallowed Ground | 2 |
| Uncle Tim | 3 |
| Creators | 5 |
| Jinja | 6 |
| Sorceress | 7 |
| Joyriding | 8 |
| The Storm Of Creation | 11 |
| Falling Apart | 12 |
| The Academy | 14 |
| The Footballer in the Square | 15 |
| Following | 16 |
| Reclaiming the Years | 17 |
| Blow Up The Dam | 18 |
| The Rock-Me Timing Bang | 19 |
| Weapons Of Mass Distraction | 21 |
| School | 22 |
| I Want It | 23 |
| The Awakening Of The Tribe | 24 |
| There Will Be Poets | 26 |
| St. George's Day | 27 |
| Spirit & Letter | 29 |
| The Great Rift Valley | 30 |
| On Coming To Power | 31 |
| Lock Me In | 32 |
| Find Me | 33 |
| Goddess | 34 |
| Search | 35 |
| A List Of British Place Names | 36 |

| | |
|---|---|
| Vote | 37 |
| Panma | 39 |
| Already | 40 |
| Pope's Tower, Stanton Harcourt | 42 |
| Dungeons | 43 |
| True Breath | 44 |
| Memory Tree | 45 |
| Logos | 46 |
| Answering Nechterne | 48 |
| Dying Wishes | 49 |
| Visitor | 51 |
| Skenfrith Castle | 53 |
| To Change | 54 |
| Burn This Page | 55 |
| She Thanks Him | 56 |
| Neuromemo | 58 |
| The Revolution Of Revelations | 60 |
| Johnny 600 | 61 |
| Nature Poem | 63 |
| Home Comforts | 64 |
| Dragon Song | 65 |
| Horse Whispering in the MIC | 68 |
| A Passer-By Demands Another Miracle | 70 |
| Page & Stage | 71 |
| Fire | 72 |
| Bwindi Impenetrable National Park | 74 |
| Walk Out | 77 |
| Sunday Morning | 78 |
| Eastbourne Cliffs | 79 |
| If Everyone Did | 81 |

## Acknowledgements

Many thanks to the editors of the following publications for first printing some of these poems:

*Acumen, Blade, Outposts, Magma, Iota, Fire, The Interpreter's House, Staple, New Hope International, Tears In The Fence, Poetry Nottingham International, Poetry Monthly, Haiku Quarterly, Caduceus, Kindred Spirit, Urthona, Psychopoetica, Doors, Wire, Rustic Rub, Candelabrum, City Writings, Tandem* and *Purple Patch*.

'Jinja' also appeared in *Earth Songs* (ed. Peter Abbs, Green Books 2002), and 'Fire', 'Eastbourne Cliffs' and 'Already' appeared in the anthology *Into the Further Reaches* (ed. Jay Ramsay, PS Avalon 2007)

A massive thank you to all the people who have inspired, supported, encouraged and believed in me, especially Becky for opening worlds; David for creating them; Angus for igniting and shaping them; Sirish for conjuring them; Tascha for letting them fly; Christina for drawing them in; Ann for seeing beyond them; Abe for teaching me to listen to them; Angel, Sandra, Chris & Rakhee, Hugo and Janette Steel for keeping them spinning; Peter Abbs, Jay Ramsay and Jane Holland for showing me more; Marcus Lyon, Chris Scholey, Sir John Hegarty, Jeremy Hinton, Sarah Sanders and Peter Clayton for sharing and gifting them; Hugo Grenville, Stephen Barlow, Steve B-K and Rohan Freeman for transforming them; Daddy, Tessa, Sonia, Zandra, Simon & Caroline for enthusing and caring about them; Jill Foster and all at Naomi House for letting them dance; all the children and all the teachers and carers who make them sing; Laurence and Elizabeth for being them, and for being mine; my mother, whispering from the other side of them; and finally to William Sieghart, without whom they and their mountains would never have moved. As for the spirit between worlds and between lines, I only hope that at least the sounds and silences of my words speak for her unspeakable power eloquently enough.

## We Have Come

We have come not to shout, but to listen;
Not to hoard, but to share;
Not to lash out, but to calm;
Not to cover up, but to lay bare.

We have come not to suffocate, but to touch;
Not to dictate, but to understand;
Not to hold back, but to unleash—
Not to shrink, but to expand.

We have come not to shadow, but to colour;
Not to conquer, but to embrace;
Not for ourselves, but for the other—
Not to silence, but to give voice.

## Hallowed Ground

Can truth, like jewels, be suddenly found?
In a dream the words lit up my mind:
*To ignite the fellowship of hallowed ground.*

What does it mean, this eerie sound?
Is it Time itself I hear unwind?
Can truth, like jewels, be suddenly found?

Our planet-threads will fray, unwound,
My task, perhaps, to weave and bind,
To ignite the fellowship of hallowed ground:

One day to see the teachers crowned,
The wheelchairs walk, the killers kind:
Can truth, like jewels, be suddenly found?

Our star shines still as we go round—
From that vast flame the spark I'll find
To ignite the fellowship of hallowed ground.

In storms of mind we run aground;
To the solar wind still blinkered, blind.
Truth will, like jewels, be suddenly found
To ignite the fellowship of hallowed ground.

# Uncle Tim

I never saw him happy again.
Jumping across the field with his briefcase
Perhaps, for a moment, he found it.
He should have grown a garden in this place.

I blame his father, mostly.
Years of exams and rigid sums
Because the old man had to be sure:
He should've listened to his mum.

She shared his silence and his love
Of harebell, primrose, fuchsia dawns:
Every spare minute of his early days
Was among the oaks and Richmond fawns.

But the father was strong;
*And each root must be paid for
In pounds and pence; and pain
Is the testing life we're made for!*

He should have climbed the oak,
But his father barked him down:
*Life's too precious for risks*
He said, only anger in his frown.

He took the path his father wished,
But my child's eye could tell
Each family picnic in the park
Was a subtle, breathless hell

Where he'd remember what he wanted
And he'd want to tell us all—
But he'd whisper me round, and show me
How the leaves swell up and fall.

And so one day I asked him
In the park at the end of the day:
*Why do you work in an office?*
*Why don't you run away?*

And he shrieked like a child
Unleashed into the heavy rain,
Jumping across the field with his briefcase.
I never saw him happy again.

He came quietly back and I started
To talk about rare plants and the people at Kew,
But he carefully steered the subject around
And asked what I wanted to do.

I wanted what he'd never had;
And more so when I saw his still face.
He should have grown a garden: he should
Have grown his garden in this place.

# Creators

Neatly placed on their appointed shelves,
Prize vegetables glitter like crown jewels.
As if they'd grown the bloody things themselves,

Owners of bulbous marrows measure their lives
By volume, width and weight. What fools!
Neatly placed on their appointed shelves

Sprouts assume a pride outside their little selves:
Another purple-veined face gloats and drools—
As if they'd grown the bloody things themselves.

Whatever time or pesticides this prize involves,
Something's forgotten in the winning and the rules.
Neatly placed on their appointed shelves,

First and second onion inflame the blood, the wives
Exchanging poison recipes, then kicking like mules
As if they'd grown the bloody things themselves.

So doctors are Gods when the patient survives;
And designer babies, spliced by researchers' tools,
Neatly placed on their appointed shelves—
As if they'd grown the bloody things themselves.

# Jinja

Though the boys selling Coke at Jinja,
the source of the Nile, have never heard of Egypt,
kingfishers know to point their bills like telescopic sights
and dive; emerge with silver in their beak,
and the perfume of the Nile in their feathers.

At the river's edge, above the stagnant pool,
red dragonflies advertise their passion;
ignore the disappointment of water
burned to dust at the margins,
never to flow on the great journey.

Flies bright as rubies
move in binary waves
across the river's silver plains:
moving to the rhythms of their race,
if they pierce the river's veil, they drown.

What watches me, beyond the veil?
What watches all the rivers
gliding through my heart?
At the end of my journey,
what sea, what planet waits for me?

In the kayak of my mind I set off
with the faith of horizons, not knowing
what rapids or falls of fire I face, or what
canyons and chasms, what echoes
in what dried-out beds await.

Yet I hear only the rivers and seas turning their wheel;
sense this is no time to question the wisdom
of water, nor the source of all that flows.
I only know these eyes, the sudden dive,
the joy of flight with silver in my beak.

## Sorceress

'I am a spring,' she says.
'I am the source.'

Come down then, down to my river—
flow through me—

trickle through the startled light
of my meadows—
these petals so curved, the pollen so moist.

This sorceress, she moves me.

Slowly she sighs an ember breath.
Fingers curve their grace on flesh
and my smile is sabre-tooth
and the beast bends in the deep cavern—

frenzy of fire on flint-cut walls
and my hide is in hackles—
bristle of nerve and sinew
roar of muscle and pulse
crush of a whisper

and agony—

the dawn sigh.

This sorceress, she moves me.

In the gasp of cooling dew
she turns

and we settle
like hands in prayer
into us.

# Joyriding
*for Scott Waring*

> *The only sin is to limit the is*
> —Richard Bach

A car isn't just the spark plugs and the engine,
the absorbers and the wheels:
it's the idea of travel, the thrill of speed,
the E-type sculpture; all the wacky beered-up
dreamings that led to the gasp of Ferrari Dino ...

Yes, I suppose a car *is* just an A to B machine.
But what about these curves?
Won't you take her for a spin,
screech Silverstone corners,
sail your love's long hair at 150?

No, I can't say you're wrong. A car *is* just a car.
But can it drive round Le Mans on its own?
What about the invisible sparks and atomic combustions,
the way it sways out of corners,
its torque and thrust and racing lines,
its beastly rumbling zorp ... ?

Yes, it *can* just be a Focus or a Golf or a Vectra,
something that takes us from A to B.
Simple as life or death.
But aren't there more letters than A and B?

What, that's what's coming out of my mouth right now?
Just a string of letters making sounds that die ... ?
I can't deny that.
But aren't I also trying to make words,
make sense, get inside your mind?

The car has evolved from rolling stone to lightning,
like our minds. You can open your eyes
wherever you choose. You can live on an island
where you only ever need to walk or you can live
in a world where the green cars of the new time
ghost across the seas like breath. You can walk in the circle
of your own tracks, or you can follow your desire
into the cockpit of your dream flycar
and rocket to the edges of Orion.
The wonder and the technology is all there.
The true science is all in place.
Nobody alive or dead has ever seen the whole picture;
but that doesn't mean there isn't one there.

Who gave you eyes? These gates into new worlds,
or, unconnected, these slimy marbles?
How does an embryo know how to grow
its own fingers, or develop its logical arguments?
Why does the earth move in circles
and not scream off like an unknotted balloon?

We're like islanders in a drugged haze,
rolling pineapples in the sand, stumbling
from one coconut grove to the next,
mumbling enthusiasm for the shuffle of feet.

So why not? Dive into the cockpit, step on the fire
in the Z-type of tomorrow—imagine the ultimate
torque and curve, and the fire'll be singing in your skull;
you'll see the pistons through the bonnet, feel the speed
ripple your face; you'll dream the shape and praise
the beauty, feel the atoms pulsing to your beat
as your heart hits the ton in the shock of a blink . . .

And when you finally reach it,
that final speedtrial at the edge of time—
not until beyond lightspeed will you know . . .

and in that final blazing through to stillness—
when man and car and fire are one—
you'll be lit up forever, like an imperishable star.

# The Storm Of Creation

Thunder—
Two continents
of rock collide.

Lightning—
A crack
in the eggshell sky.

Rain—
Cleansing
for the sacrifice.

She cuts off your mind
with a golden sword

and to the drum
of the infinite drum

you hatch
in the healing moss;

and dried
by the lovelight of suns

you fly out beyond
the outer skies

to explode
your star of love,

sending out
the storm of your seed

to wake new wings
to the highest skies of fire.

# Falling Apart

Batman? Gandhi? Bruce Willis? Jesus? Superman?
Never showed up. Innocence crushed in a million tons of ash
And not a phoenix to be seen. Only a flying great white shark
With teeth of fire and blood, cloned for destruction
In the black hole egos of the wounded
Where beauty is smothered in suffocating darkness.

Two thousand hearts torched and torn in hellfire,
Smashed by a hundred floors of ash-thundering steel and stone.

But some, they jumped—some, hand in hand—
Dreaming they might wake before they hit the ground.
They *hit* the ground. Felt the nightmare concrete punch of dust.

Spiderman? Jesus? No sign. No miracle airlock rescue.
No mother and son reunited in great hug of hope.... Hope ...

Hope is a candle, burning inside; and now spinning in whirlwinds
Of light as supernova hearts explode open at the edge of the universe
And here on earth simultaneously; incredible miracle of the possible,
Light you don't get burned by to become the sun in your inner sky
And scorch to shame those who *think* they've found the flame—
They're playing the old, cold game of nail the lovers down.

God forgive them for they know what they do!
*Father, forgive them, for they know not what they do*

And a light uncurls this fist to a palm as we remember
We are in good hands—the only hands that will hold us forever
With the tenderness always of a newborn in the strong grip
Of his weeping father—the hand that will be there waiting for you,
Taking away the pain of your fall

As two ordinary superheroes jump out of burning hell
Just to know the brief wild freedom of leaving
Their slow motion skyscraper life hand in hand —

Just to open the eyes of the whole world
And show that only love holds us together.

## The Academy

They made words and sense here:
Orders and borders and morals and fear.
Not fetres or beat and rimmonson chins
Or litanies plastered in muggings of Pimm's

Where strawhats inspire at the burdicled view—
Where innerskull icepins inglisten with blue—
Transfoxing old bookworms of mortarboard chins
Who with oratored chalk and warblegame sins

Demysticate joy and the sting of the song—
The ploy of the noise in the blaze of the bong.
But oh jingle be phrased, they have lost the boook
Forbidding all kinds of gobbledegook!

The gobbledefractal buzzing of moons
Rotating the truth in our quantumleap spoons—
The tango of fins in the grail of the deep
In the middle of minds where the phoenix can't sleep

And volcanoes have wings and a labyrinth hatch—
Where galaxies spin on the whack of a match
To dazzle the learned, whose red-adair wits
Now start to hiphop to the rhythmical bits

And tie up their chi with an ecstable smile—
Flashing their bulbs in the novabang style—
Mid the mare of this mash that mangled their scheme
And flooded with gold the old dry academe!

# The Footballer in the Square
*for Andy, Chris, Will & Paddy*

The young boys show off their skills
And keep the ball from the youngest one
In the square of Puerto de Mogan.

All around the families are smiling,
Breathing slowly as the children learn.

The youngest footballer squeaks like a puppy
As another cunning swerve foils his longing
For a touch of the ball. Enter stage right

A humble face of nineteen with feet of light like bells
That dance a spell to steal the ball, and flick it back
And up and kick, kick, kick; quick balance
On the neck and flick; and trap like a gift at the feet

Of the youngest boy, whose eyes widen like a sky.

The other boys bow as the humble face walks away.

# Following

If I am killed, do not assume
That life has lost its innocence;
If my nerves or cells cannot resume
Their work, do not take offence.

I always knew how brief we are,
So learned the patterns of the Sun:
Was there ever any blazing star
Not framed by dark? There is none.

We curse ourselves who curse the world
Where love awaits, and silken days:
I saw the spider's magic pearled,
An abacus of hidden ways—

Love lay beneath my fears and schemes;
Even now I follow, weaving through my dreams.

## Reclaiming the Years

How can so much be lost?
Not a smell nor a touch from the years
I know my mother was there.

I look at the silver buttons on the Mustang radio
in disbelief—they just punched me
with a screech, and I can feel my mouth
filling up with something.
I wish I remembered her more than the pain
in my gums; or the radio broadcast—
a child beaten to death for crying.

Looking across into her eyes I see the light
of reassurance and that wryness puzzling to the child:
I say those years are numb but even in my dreams
the roses are not scent but paint, and the furnace
does not leave you blistered as you wake.

I have no call to cry out now: there is no pain
as I observe my teeth, mute and wet-rooted
on the dashboard. I clack them together now
and feel the rocking of her laughter,
her scented kiss neither dream nor memory but here.

She looks up, pearled and nineteen,
from an image I dared not face till now:
as I tend light and pour sound
she watches, wry and proud,
and loves the songs we make.

## Blow Up The Dam

Blow up the dam, release
the living streams of language!

A trickle of syllables soon flows
Into runnels in the rhythm of the rivers,
Roars in a flood of mind down
To the ancient truth of seas.

Plunge into the seas beyond!
Pour the cycles of water and fire
Onto the page, into your throat—
Blow up the dam that separates
You from me, who are one skull,
Woven in a perfect web of gold.

Release the living streams of light!
Dive into the oceans of *this* world—
Tend to the unwashed hands,
The tenderness of the predator—
Swim naked with the porpoise,
Sing in the cathedrals of the sharks—
Pulse, like the squid, with all the spectrum

And you, who lived half your life
In the desert beneath the dam—
Who feared the little drop of you
Would evaporate in fire

Are now one mighty sea

Clinging tight to the face
Of the planet you love.

# The Rock-Me Timing Bang

Acoustic tuning-seers,
Here's the rock-me timing bang!
It's like erogenous cinematics
Or intravenous slang—
It's the slam in the roll
And the scream in the fall,
Or the telescopic purity
Of a starlit crystal ball

That reads the ley-lines
Through the on-lines
Where the rhythm
Seeks sublime . . .
Or sees the white cliffs
Shatter in the clatter
Of a time whose chime
Isn't chaste, which flatters

The cut-and-paste method—
Where the predator is chased
Method—'His tale is a waste'
Method—'til the facile are faced
By the green cries of felicity,
And the gold tribes of the free—
Just as the sun wakes, singing
*Wedlock isn't padlock, so be*

*Glad of motherbabe*, and the soul says
Yes, the whole will bless
Capital 'W' for Word, so you'll not fall down
The professor-hole, the cold chess
Of the mind's endgame—
You're here to find the way through,
The flipside breakthrough
Of me and you (*the original version*)

Before the subversion of flow,
The go. stopped. by. inhibitors—
The pharmaceutical *do-not-enter-the-centres*
The velociraptors
Of your holy soulstrings—
As the men who think they *own* love
Don their rubber gloves for the inner
Inspection: yes, introspection doves

Will section you, and sever
The connection between me and you,
Who are one body, but defeatable
In parts—their mind is a ruse
For vivisection! So stay alive, walk out
Of the cage, feel the light-
Rage of the sage say the slang
Of the timing bang's not over quite

Yet, because the epigram
Of hexagrams is who I am
And twenty grams of what I am
Will say to all the radio hams
Don't split it up, or the heart will
Jam jam jam jam jam jam

Jam n' go with the fireflow
Of go-river flow-river go-
River flow, and melt the,
Melt the, glacial snow—
So your truth, and your truth,
And your truth, will know . . .

# Weapons Of Mass Distraction

You will be famous

You will fall deeply in love
When you sign just here

You will become rich
And make us richer

You will be made comfortable
And will not complain

You will find desire
And lose your soul

You will buy freedom
Just as you sell it

You will feel excitement
And know the pain of transience

You will become clever
As you are made stupid

You will be hoovered by lust
And never know the cleanness
Of spring

You will be famous

Love will come and go

You will be dust

# School

In the crowded rooms of day, armed
with strict grammars and bent smiles,
the teacher is bemused by his own frail
platitudes no sky can twist itself into—

elsewhere, edging beyonds, he sees
the gifts he wishes he could give.
Through tempests in his eyes
the clouds accelerate between worlds,

the light is pouring from his fingers—
healing beyond grammars, light
beyond logic; with these gifts, young
minds could share the visions

of this night, and they too could fly
beyond the numbered asteroids,
share with us these ancient stars
sprinkling our souls like confetti.

## I Want It

I want it to sound right
To whisper and reverberate
Round the curves of your heart.

I want it to touch you
To sail its fingerprints
Around the globe of your breast.

I want it to flick that switch
In the attic cupboard
Of your childhood dream.

I want it to smell the heath
That threw back your head
In the shock glance of my tongue.

I want it to stun you—
To wrap its wires around your secrets
And sizzle like lightning.

Yes, and then I want it to burn you
To hurl you up at night
And let you light the world.

Then I want it to cool you—
To trail its slow cube of ice
Across your nose, nipples, navel, toes.

And then, in the silent balm of lying back,
As the world walks its thin, loose rope,
I want it to say *I love you.*

## The Awakening Of The Tribe

In the dark and beery silence, something tribal.
I could sense it in their bellies, something tribal.
I knew what they had come for—
I saw the iron bar—
I smelt the life unspoken, something tribal.

My sister sat so silent, but she smelt it.
The roots—rooted tugging—we all felt it.
They had touched her, they had soiled her
And by God these evil worms
Would feel pain—the pain inside—as they had dealt it.

So simply my father said
The adult words *Now go to bed.*
So many times he'd walked blindfold past it—
Past the cropped heads and the slurred threats,
Just for us. But this was different.
Only the old ways would do now.

Thirty male bellies full of stout.
One little sister full of pain.
Eight cropped heads laughing loud.
Only the old ways would do now.

A gathering of purpose, something tribal.
The iron bar of vengeance, something tribal.
My father simply knew, knew exactly what to do,
The old, old justice, something tribal.

There are orders, there are rules, something tribal.
There are lovers, there are fools, something tribal.
And in folding back the years I see folding back my fears
Thirty stout-breathed vigilantes, marching tribal.

There are limits, there are bonds
Iron bars, not magic wands—
And my father put things straight,
Something tribal.

I never even ask how they set about the task,
How they beat the rod of justice on that night.
But I know that when they set upon the table in the night
That iron bar in light that it was bent—
That the old ways had put my sister right.
And God forbid I ever lose the old ways of truth
Drumming like iron bars onto damned flesh—
Neither lose my strong and silent brothers
Coming together in a great gathering—
The gathering of justice, truly tribal.

## There Will Be Poets
*a version of Rilke's first Sonnet to Orpheus*

A tree is rising, there—it's a miracle!
God sings a tall tree in your ear
And all is still. In this lyric, all
Begins *now*; all is changing *here*—

Animals from the silence come into the clear
From dens and nests, into the open wood.
It wasn't *guile* that brought them here,
Or let them breathe so softly: they could

Only come to *listen*. Howls and roars they found
Too limited for their hearts. And though, before this,
The tiniest hut had held what was heard here—
An airless place of longing and fear
With a rickety old door for an entrance—

Now you build them cathedrals in their sense of sound.

# St. George's Day

I'm proud to admit—gosh! Aren't you proud to be
Bobby Charlton, Mini Cooper, Monty Python?
To be alive in this green and pleasant mad mix of
Wayne Rooney, Amir Khan, Robin Hood, Leaves On The Line,
Stonehenge, E-type Jaguars, Marmite, The Clash?
This Michael (or Wilfred) Owen, Johnny Rotten, Camilla, Charlie,
Paul McCartney, Barmy Army, Ode to a Nightingale?
Vindaloo! Ecowarriors. Sol Campbell. Vivienne Westwood.
Darwin, Shelley, Newton, Wembley; creative and financial
Bobby Moore of the Globe?

Oh the real ale, Frank Bruno, Wimbledon Queues, Ted Hughes:
The great bard's well 'ard: Vinny Jones, The Rolling Stones . . .
Avebury. Middle Order Batting Collapse. Bohemian Rhapsody, Chaps?
Page 3, Rolling Hills, Satanic Mills—*Last Of The Summer Wine* . . .
I May Be Gone Some Time . . . Reach For the Sky! You Are The Weakest Link,
Goodbye! Poor Old Toad, Wrong Kind Of Snow; Quiet Desperation;
Help Me Out O Corporation . . . 7.13 to Waterloo Station of it all . . .

This realm of Cod 'n' Chips, Mr. Bean, Johnathon Woss, Wall's Ice Cream,
Marquee Weddings, *The Beano*, Bluebells, Church Bells, 180! Swing Low,
Sweet Chariots Of Fire—it's the *taking part*; it's the TAKING APART!
Goodness Gracious Me! BBC, OBE, I'm Free! Three Lions On A Shirt—
Strawberry Fields Forever: Transient, Trance, Rave, Techno,
Emo Trainspotting; Welcome To The House Of Fun (And The Drugs
Don't Work) Kate Moss Bros, Becks 'n' Posh, who gives a toss?
But the Wonderful Thing About Tiggers is Magic Roundabout
Hedgerows and Chainsaws Brixton Riots Tellytubbies, The Jam, The Jam!
Ordering Organic Cucumbers On the Internet; Camelot becomes a Lottery,
And the Winner is . . . Stephen Lawrence's Mum, and Dad's Army,
The Dark Side Of The Mooning Out Of Cars, Gary Numan—
the Numinous . . . !

*Imagine All The People Living Life* beyond national identity—
the you & me connected beyond national identity . . .

(Well, everybody needs a bosom for a pillow)—
the all-admitted (*no exclusions*) of you & me
watching those feet in ancient times walk upon
England's mountains green—or silver in the lake,
Excalibur! And Arthur, whose hand takes the sword
like a thorn from your heart—round table, fresh start:
To Be Or Not To Be The Example Of Nations?
Defenders Of Faith always look on the bright side of
Chaos/Order/Chaos/Order/Duality/Unity/Order—
Butterfly Wingbeat of the Individual Gesture:
Why Leave That Candle Unlit?
Left, Right, Middle Path!
Sprinting along the fence to the Golden City—
Egg, Sperm; Miracle of Life . . . !
*You May Say I'm A Dreamer*—
Milton, Blake, Kevin Keegan . . .
So I'm not the only one . . .
. . . and aren't you proud to be
—The Power Of You & Me!
*. . . nor shall our swords sleep in our hands*
Alive in the Living Word
Of the Here & Now,
The Beat Of the Burning Heart
Blazing Once More in the Deep
As the Lightning Seeds Burst

And Scatter a Bright New Hope
In this Happy Mixed Breed
Of Emerging Gods
Awaking New-Inspired At Last
Upon this Precious Earth,
This Blossoming Realm,
This Wild & Holy Rose Garden Of An Island,
This . . . ENGLAND!

## Spirit & Letter

They want us to conform to the old forms,
Not light up some firestorm, some higher
Principality beyond all formality: worms
Are what they think we are, and dust. Liar

Is what fire must call them: they may be tall,
But watch them all plummet from the summit
When we speak in pentecosts and say the fall
Is their fault: they hear the tune but don't strum it.

They're balloons, they won't win: we've got the pin
And we will use it. You can't abuse it . . . these gifts
Shouldn't be rifts between us, but connections. Sin
Is a rich man hoarding—yet see how the shaker sifts

In the rhythmical pan the sand from the radiant gold:
They've found the sound; but silence can't be sold.

# The Great Rift Valley

Vultures stare down on the great valley.
The first pillar of sky fell here,
left its print as long as Africa.

On the plains below zebra kick dust into the shadows
as evening broods, pregnant with rain. Gazelle hairs stiffen
ready for the fall, but a seventh sense alerts the vultures
to a deeper darkening: they steal away in shrieks beyond the clouds

as lightning lurches with bent claws,
sizzling its pain like the death chair: thunder cracks
like test tubes pressed too far: lions convulse,
wild tongues frothing with twisted chemistries:

flung down from darkness, vast webs of wires, chains
and cables writhe and clasp the valley edges,
clamping their suckers like tapeworm, heaving the edges in:
in the madness of shadows zebra gnash through their own
hooves, teeth racing like chainsaws: gazelles sprout fangs,
rip apart their young as the valley sides bulldoze closed
in ending's roar like the Red Sea roaring in.

Wires winch to final tightness like vagina lips stitched.
Last little lumps of earth teeter into the slit, nearly silent.

From an edge, two dying zebra limp out
like insects from death's demented lips:
into the hell-dark mouth the vultures swoop,
feasting in the deep dark on bent meat and baked blood:

soon bloated, lonely in the dark circles of their tribe,
they flap awkwardly between the silent carcasses,
remembering wings wide as the world—
the brightness of blood in the sun—
dreaming of what the first pillars held high.

# On Coming To Power
*for Gordon*

The earth's in a spin, as the still man knows.
But why curse the thorns? Remember the rose
Opening in the always—enter in:
No one here denies the sacrifice and sting,
The rare courage that welcomes in the light.
When we hear, we should follow it, the cry
In the wilderness so easily ignored.
Grace pours out of space in the living rain,
Rusting the guns' rage and nurturing the grain.
We can't build on sand, its lies and its lore—
In the drought, we're grateful for what's been stored.
An ancient shining awakes the new sense;
Gifts ignite the deep heart's intelligence
As the arc above the ark whispers *Less is more.*

## Lock Me In

Lock me in, I don't mind:
This is no punishment.
Perhaps you love the drama
Of the keys, the measured slams.
For me it is music, a tuning up
For the opera you cannot hear.

I do not fold myself up on my bed
Like a foetus in the dark sea.
I pause and gaze at the window,
Opening like a porthole.

Its opening is my ritual,
And climbing out my courage—
Until I stand on the roof
As a child of the sky
Where the clouds have no keys
And the invisible stars
Are diamonds hiding in the darkness
Of my little room—

And though it is day, they sparkle now
And I can see squirrels fly in moonlight
And porpoise surf in the tanker waves

And I can see the storm of my mother's face
Calm to a smile.

Lock me in, I don't mind.
I don't believe you mean me harm.
If you really wanted to punish me
You'd take away the sky.

# Find Me

Find me the geneticist
Who can grow a baobab tree
From his own seed
That will outlast human history

Find me the sorcerer
Who can craft the filigree
Of a rose's petals
Century after century

Find me the electrician
Who can ignite the star
That lights a million galaxies
And shows you who you are

Find me the psychologist
Who can make a man free
And brave enough to forgive
Those who've nailed him to a tree

Find me the brain surgeon
Who can find the channel
That connects a child
To the centre of heaven

Find me the astronaut
Who waits beyond time
For a single soul to begin
The long journey home

Find me a human being
And I will come
Running to embrace you
Like a long-lost son

## Goddess

She keeps the fire alive and knows no lust.
Dust she has seen, and champions the stranger.

Arrange her slowly and love will show you
True as a child, the placenta of truth:
Truth to nourish the unborn world.

Whirled in the pool of her cupped hands,
Lands shine apple-still in a sea of glass.

Ask, and her tasks will be assigned you.
Behind you, death swarms—but before
Imploring, you leap bravely out of water's sleep,

Keeping calm, for her breath is starlight:
Knights in a daze are waking at the fall,
Calling to be burned by the breath of her brand
In the land of the star-tongued messengers.

# Search

I walked through the hidden libraries
Searching for the book of me.
Every book in the half-light
Promised much, gold letters
On leather spines, shining titles
Like *The Secret Of Scarastavore*
Or *The Helixes of Alexandria*.
When I opened them, only shadows
Patterned the blank parchment,
And the dust fell like powdered bone.

After many miles of darkness
Listening to my heels on the stone slabs
I saw a copper light, then a small domed room.
In the centre, laid out like a body,
Was a book the length of a man,
Radiating green and gold.
Inside it, a scarab beetle edged across a page,
Dripping gold from its mouth.
It formed a large circle, and inside it the shape
Of Mannaz, the Viking Rune: symbol of joy
And joy reversed, the balance of heart and mind.

Looking into its light the room turned gold,
And then the whole library was lit up, and from above
I could see it was a vast labyrinth laid out like a golden web
And every book shone like dew.

I listened to chance, which led me
To the brightest book of all
And, like a sun rising, it opened
On this page, still being written.

# A List Of British Place Names

Thundersley
Tempar
Upsettlington
Yelling

Tiptoe
Calmesden
Lulsley
Healing

Nancledra
Drumwhindle
Rora
Malaclete

Rescassa
Thornfalcon
Soundwell
Merrymeet

Ring O'Bells
Wordsley
Ayres of Selivoe
Warbleton
Rubery
Perranzabuloe

Scarastavore
Babbacombe
Combebow
Ryme Intrinseca

Soham

Lockerbie

Dunblane

# Vote

War is a war of what you would die for: love evolving, nature overcoming nature. But we are the prey of desire of the day, the keep-you-angry newspapers; imprisoned in a skull, fearful of all fundamentalists, foreigners, next door neighbours. We live to complain in late night emails or on tiny soapboxes in the comfort of our own virtual home, voting once every five years for this lie or that deception.

Vote with the rhythm of your time and the healing in your hands. Vote with nothing but the truth, the language of autumn leaves, the storm before the calm.

Leave blank the reverence for the journalist, celebrity, the gadget, television. And why fill the box beside *origin*? Simply fill the air with the curved resonance of tabla and dulcimer, kalimba, ney and mandolin; the understanding after a triangle is struck ...

Put all your thinking to one side for the child whose eyes are talking in questions, but whose mouth is a fishing boat stranded in mud, waiting for the tide of your patient listening. The war is a war of what you would die for.

Vote with your fingers, your burning mind. Wrap yourself in Semtex, in electrical wires, fuses and detonators; wrap yourself in the high explosives of Love: then, with a great prayer, blow yourself up and everything with you—blow up the hoarding and the legalese, the greed and the clinging, the shut-out clauses and the gossip, the too-far-gone-to-cares and I-can't-do-thats, the love of only the like-minded and the remote control. See the smithereens of what we all thought so important. And as the air slowly clears, a breeze like wisdom finds new space to breathe ... to breathe of the suicide of love, to breathe and walk like more-than-men past our broken nature into the radiant human nature that will outshine everything you've ever feared.

Vote for something bigger than fear and words and knowing. Vote for questions in your answers. Vote for something more subtle than voting. Say yes to listening to the music of your neighbour: how many languages can you laugh in? How many languages can you die in? Say yes to living—and dying —for Love.

# Panma

There was a room in my house I'd never
Been to, and my grandfather was there.

It had high ceilings and sparkled like a cabaret.
He entertained us with witty rhythms
From the throne of his piano stool.

I was so thrilled to see him. I had to
Remind my wife that he had died.
His every word was a blessing.
It was bliss to hear the stern man
Laugh and sing like a child.

I told him his house and gardens
Were in good hands, and he wept for his father.
We hugged for the first time.
He was frail as bone china,
But wanted *me* to be comfortable.

Waking robbed me of his smiling moustache
And deep, unhurried voice.
Then I heard it once more :
*Build from the inner life.*

There was a room in my house I'd never
Been to, and my grandfather was there.

# Already

> *Live as though the time were here*
> — Nietszche

*It's already here*

The silver web of silence glows like mercury
And in your ear the swallows shriek in the soft rain
Above the temple bells humming like starlight
And inside, like a golden bullet fired inside a speeding
Golden bullet, the spirit moves faster than science

*It's already here*

In my pocket enough power to turn a city of love
Into little pieces of people falling like leaves of blood,
In my heart enough love to split my body
Into many parts, so that my neighbour may die,
So that my neighbours may be free

*It's already here*

The children play in a paradise of money
Where they grow and grow and vote for fame;
Or the sudden silver of the hidden water
Where the child dives into the world
That God sees too

*It's already here*

Our fingers speaking in tongues
Our bodies trembling with the invisible
Curtains opening in the desert city
Windows opening in the desert city
We are walking in a wind

*It's already here*

Our wings are not moving yet we are carried
Our wings are moving and we can dip and turn
And dance in this wind, we can see the valleys of a breeze
And the mountain ranges of the breath, breathing
To be God's everywhere and all at once

*It's already here*

# Pope's Tower, Stanton Harcourt
*for the Gascoignes*

Visitors come to see the pane of glass that bears his name.
Through it he'd seen young lovers struck by lightning,
Remarked that the chaste had died of the clap.

In this chapel he'd raged at the organ
With his rhythmic fire in a chair
Carved to fit the hunch of his back.

My sister was christened here, her marriage
Blessed. Behind the altar a thousand years
Of family names observe our notable moments.

I walked here with her across formal gravel.
School shoes scratched the bowed flagstones.
My father in a green waterproof jacket

Towered between us in the doorway—
Still as the effigies—and faced the coffin.
He squeezed us into the folds of his coat

Cold to my ears, screeching like knife on glass,
Then silent as in numb surrender I listened
To my father's calm in its coat of stone

Until the tower broke into a primal heaving sob,
Shaking the stones and the organ pipes
As the names of a thousand years flowed away.

## Dungeons

Will death be another dungeon,
With chains and a rack and some bars,
Or will the heavy cell door open
To the perfume of night and the stars?

Our days can be gentle torture
When we crave what we cannot own;
Hoarding our scraps of mould,
Afraid of being alone.

But the oak and the lark know better—
They follow the will of the seed.
Their beauty is being themselves,
Their nature is their creed.

And if we listen to our nature,
Our skull becomes the sky—
The wind becomes our medium,
And an answer whispers by

Saying 'Death in life is the dungeon
And the cell door is our heart—
Open it up to the night,
See the stars begin to part.'

# True Breath
*a version of Rilke's third Sonnet to Orpheus*

A god can do it. But how can mere men
Walk this burning wire, singing to the light?
Our minds are out of tune. Cathedrals will never be built
For poets as long as the old battles rattle and din.

Because poetry, as *she* sees it, is not about ego,
The flattery and the glitter, all that jazz.
Poetry is the event itself, for God's own ears.

When will we learn to be *alive?*—When God shows
The seas and trees and stars waking us *from the inside!*

It's not the flush and crush of love you knew as a boy,
Though her ringing bells once flung that mouth open wide.
Such fizz falls so flat, so fast. It's time to move on:
The true breath of song resounds with far sweeter joy;
... a carefree canticle; a wind rippling on the sea of God.

## Memory Tree

Bold words unsigned, head-high
inside the hollow oak on the heath:
thick splats of red paint, dried in drips.

In winter match-lit shadows
I read them out to you:
TO THE MEMORY OF MY UNBORN CHILD.

We walked on, lingering
at the carved declarations
of love on the beech's trunk.

Far from the heath I watched
the spring hills swelling, marvelled
at a young oak hugged tight with bark:

suddenly I saw her tears,
and the red paint mournful as spilt blood
lit up by her solemn candle

and her praying inside the oak's empty womb
as ritual blood and ritual light
knitted their healing around her:

easing her pain I hope, the oak
wrapping her up in its grace
like the first mother.

# Logos

Logo's a no-go that throws the flow and blows the globe so dough's a dodo so-and-so disease; please squeeze the trees of all their sap, suck out the fish, hear the food chain snap, freeze all the love, put desire on tap, keep the good people down in the poverty trap; I say old chap, d'you write to *The Times* in rap? Or the clap in the storm of alive is a slap in the face, a star falls for the grief of this place; the future's bright, the future's *blue*; what else does Love want *you* to do? You've got five seconds to go, you're so wasted crew, no wonder they're sinking the think in your thinking they're drinking you dry, first class Martini mile high, telling us we can't fly *anywhere* without them, I wonder why; but the lie isn't over till the big mama sings from the white cliffs of Dover of the wings we need to be freed from their creed; they're remixing the love life you *really* need: listen to the reed bending in the wind; forgive me mother, I've been binned; recycle my soul, let me climb to be whole, all the time I've been sold; I thought Red Bull gave me—

save me, for Red Bull is what it is, we are the slaves to all this, glued to the cave wall of all this, this is your call, all of this; watch us all fall in this bliss, breathe in the call, believe in the leaving all this, love believes in the listening bliss; time to rewind them, and then to remind them that we are all players and we'll sing our say as we play in the spray as we surf away on the waves of the star that burns and burns, is burning beyond; we must eyeball all of the pike in the pond, watch the fern turn, learn about spores and the frond, feel our hearts and minds burn in the core and beyond, we can soar, take the child out of war and beyond; better jump off the merrygostore, see beyond—

because the sun's just spun in the no-go of the logo, taking a fireblade to the knot of the flow crew: *dadading-batama-batamaloo!* so give back your heart, don't let them brand it, just stand under, yes, you can stand it! Stand under and you *will* understand it! You just hooked a marlin, don't brand it—you just hooked a marlin in the sun of the seventh seal, so reel it in, it's something *real* on the silver hook; reel it in, it's something you can *feel* on the silver hook; reel it in, bring it on board; look it in the eye, see its spike like a sword; look it in the eye, don't let them brand it: look it in the eye and you begin to under-stand it; and so, you let it go, splashing back into the nameless burning water

## Answering Nechterne

I have come
From the light at the centre
And the loneliness of the edge.

I am many names
That ring with the deep lightning
And the wisdom of white horses.

I am dovetailer,
The weaver of the white wings
And the covenant of rainbows.

I am to ignite
Fresh skies in young hearts,
To rekindle birdsong in the old.

I spring from wells
And wormholes, speaking
In flames and the songs of dolphins.

I am the son
Of a compass mother
And a navigator father.

The Christ is greater than me,
Spinning the wheel of love
And the stars, singing the silent light.

## Dying Wishes

Don't read me a poem.
Tell me what you honestly feel.
Are you scared?

You won't know what to say.
Tell me I'm being brave.
Remember something happy we shared.

Tell me I'm being brave.
See if you can make me laugh.
It's difficult to be wise.

Please, just hold my hand.
Rub the nape of my neck.
Look me in the eyes.

Take each finger, one by one,
And wrap it up
In the warmth of your hand.

Talk to me just as you always do.
Tell me about the weather—
The clouds, the sun, the trees, the wind.

Don't tell me too much about your plans.
My world is ending, so I suppose I like to think
Everyone I love has put their futures on hold.

Not that I want anyone to be sad.
I just want to feel them with me.
I never thought I'd feel so cold.

I'm tired now.
That's right, just play with my fingers.
That's lovely.

And tell me I'm being brave.
Tell me I'm being brave.

# Visitor

A poem is a dream of sound
And this is my dream—
I dream of a vast sunbird from Andromeda
Gliding to our planet on the secret
Thermal breath of stars.
The sunbird lands on Madagascar
In a frenzied din of hope and fear.
A figure descends, thin and graceful as an impala,
Its cloak of feathers the colour of fire.
The face is almost human, but shines like a wetsuit.
The eyes are stiller and deeper than a whale's.

In the clash of cameras Earth's great leader
Swells with bearded charisma and points to the sky.
His top scientists have lassoed the moon
And are winching it across for an eclipse, so their visitor
May observe the entire planet lit up by day in neon light.

The visitor takes the leader's hand and hushes him
With his sea-dark eyes. 'Please do not,' the visitor whispers.
'Please take me to the edge of your sea, to a place
where only the wind and the waves disagree.'
A young scientist with nocturnal eyes knows a place.
'By the desert. The Skeleton Coast.'

The young man takes them there, and under the first stars
The three men sit cross-legged in the sand,
Looking out at the skeletons of battered ships,
Listening to the tale of the wind and the waves.
'In your loud world' the visitor begins, 'I must tell you this.'
'The knowledge that will save you lives in sound. All the love,
The truth of happiness: all is hidden in natural sound.'

Wave after wave falls in the night.
'But what about *silence*?' the young man asks.

'The greatest secrets of all are hidden
 In the ultrasound of silence.
The power that fuels the brightest stars burns there.'

'But what must we *do*?' the leader asks.

'We shall wait patiently for dawn,
And listen to the songs of the light.'

# Skenfrith Castle
*for Christina*

Who knows what distant longing eye
Still stumbles cold through swamp and falls
To look beyond the pain and spy
The beacon's blaze on Skenfrith walls?

Who knows the end of Marcher Lords
Who, on the tumbling of the light,
Took out their secret charts to see
If their new star was still as bright?

Who knows whose faces haunt us now,
Their stony profiles sharp as swords;
Too proud in time to beg or bow,
But tender still to lovers' words?

Who knows just where our dust will fall?
What charts the lovers' final fate?
We're moved by fire, but after all,
We are the remnants in the grate.

Yet circled by this roofless tower,
Watching archers shoot the stars,
We are the fire in all its power
Spitting cinders through the bars.

## To Change

Entertainment's doing us in; coin after coin,
Pizza and Playstation, we fritter our gifts;
Ignore the cries for the flipside shift.

And so fear seeps in to numb and dull as time
Turns us from spring to corruption-slime.
The chemical smog hangs and will not lift:

There is nothing we have not interfered with.

And so we ridicule wings, the sense of sublime —
All is lottery and innuendo, lifestyle prying;
TV makeovers where nothing actually changes.

It's all so cowardly: *why are you even trying?*
Castrated voices whine: then I see the Ganges,
Golgotha, Damascus, The Dalai Lama, Beijing:

Tiananmen boys facing the tanks like angels.

## Burn This Page

Rip it out and apologise
To the poem on the other side.
It's best if it's summer, and shining,
Because you'll need a magnifying glass.

Through the thick glass
Point the sting of the captured ray
At the second 'e' of here
And try not to quiver or shake.

After ignition, as the fire twists the page,
Thank the sun quietly
For all its hard work
And its billions of burning years.

Then somewhere quiet, somewhere green,
Listen carefully as you scatter the ashes
And you might just hear the curl of the flame,
The things I was trying to say

## She Thanks Him
*for Jenni Cocking*

She thanks him each day for the tears.
He lived for just four hours,
But she thanks him each day for the tears.

They took him away
And she had no time to hold him.
But she thanks him each day for the tears.

Before he came, her life was a box.
She lived in a windowless room
And painted herself with fresh masks

Every day, bringing down
The blinds on the sky in her mind.
Now she thanks him each day for the tears.

They took him away
And she had no time to hold him.
But now each day she finds a moment

To walk with slow steps
To a chapel of rest in the sky,
Where her heart opens to the sea of light

So she can pour her love into the empty cups
Of her friends, and into her
Second child, and her third child.

In the shock of her pain — in the pain
Of that little body taken away from her,
That little miracle they could not let her hold,

[56]

She found her true body, endless
As the sky—and she carries it with her
Through the streets and rooms of her days

And she never forgets; never forgets.
She thanks him each day for the tears.
She thanks him each day for the tears.

# Neuromemo

Lonely. Skin. Dust.
Light. Lips. YES!
NO, must be careful.
One old whisper on the network tube
these days and you're downstream.

I know. I know I'll have to sink this,
but how slippery the old therapies feel
sliding over rapids, over the obscene megaliths
of the data genome.

I wish. Yes, I wish they hadn't rained
on all the old windows: what a view
of blossom bees from the French doors
and the labyrinths of lichen cities!

These wires must look like bindweed in the laser light.
I remember. I remember the pearled webs weaving,
weaving their wonder in the infinite inside.

Infinity, finity . . . this darkness is finity all right.
I hope I've lit up a few of the old frequencies.
Perhaps this phosphorescence will
brand itself onto a rare breeze, find other worlds
like our dreams were, paths on the inside
where the light is still connected,
where they're still hopeful for the hidden brain,
still inspired about the marvels of the double helix.

Who am I now? I'm black as an eyesocket
nailed into their dark dream.

I wish. I wish I could remember anger, or the bump
of my Adam's apple trembling on the stage.
There's no gold in this silence
and they drown all the people dreams.
Who was it who cried to dream again?

I used to sing what I mean
Think think think think NO

YES, I remember —
I remember being woken once . . .
there was an audience

## The Revolution Of Revelations

Petals squeezed down the barrels of Kalashnikovs was OK,
But the long division of insurrection's due for correction:
Desperate times call for inspiration out of time, a holy way
To shine the bigbang prayer of the burningsane expansion—

And so recitations of reciprocity erupt with unprecedented ferocity
And the veracity of capacity hearts is the start
Of the end of verbosity, and the festival of light in cities
And towns spreads from candle to candle, from heart

To heart; and we can hear the end of fear burning
In the turning spheres of sacred tears of falling light,
Too subtle for sense and tense; but second sighting
And the sounding light of it is true—the truth of light—

The time to fight is now, for all those guards to fall—
Bulldozing of the final wall—asleep no more.
We are too bright, too tall to fall again, too tall
Now we have shrunk upon our knees and score

The rhythmical heat of the heart of ourselves.
Pills we never knew left on darkened shelves
We take now and score the kick of who we truly are:
O Holy Ghost, you superstar! Never knew how far

The sky stretched through the old bars of who
I thought I was, who I bought I was, the stealing
Of my feelings, little thoughts of me in charge but no,
Now I am the feeling sky breathing round the world your healing.

# Johnny 600

Nose and face cracked like dried mud.
He rolls his own beside a pint of cider
And remembers the scrapyard days,
Watching the bread van through stolen binoculars.

He learned to read and write in prison
And planted a tree for her when she died.

The best years were the open prison,
Making a greenhouse from pieces
Stolen from the shoe workshop.
The marrows were gigantic;
They were the best years.

Walking through Dublin at 4 a.m.
With shoes four sizes too big for him,
Held fast by rubber bands.
No socks, of course, when he flicked
Off the big shoes and ran like hell—
Before he was caught.
The gangrene slowed him down.

He loves old cars and chess and Oscar Wilde.
He'll never beat his children
Because he remembers the pain;
Never met his Norwegian father,
But his Gran used to kneel in the gravel to pray.

His son is grand, but his daughter
Steals off him. Just like her mother.

Clearing out dead people's houses
Pays for his cider and his paper.
The smell doesn't bother him anymore.
*Perfect job for a cynic like me.*

They didn't find one body for six months.
*You should've seen the bluebottles.*
*Bluebottles the size of aeroplanes.*
He rubs tobacco between his fingers
As if he's just discovered soil.

I can't see the cracks.
Only his eyes.

## Nature Poem

If I was writing this Nature's way,
It would have to be grand and cryptic:
I'd cut root and mammal shapes into these pages
And furl them up, crumpled as mountains.
Then from the origami range
I'd pattern letters so vast
You could read the clues from Mars.

The pattern would take lifetimes
To shape, journeys through the secret land
Of dreams and the libraries of Man—
Yet even if I saw through a thousand eyes,
Past vales of death and judgment fields,
Through prophets' minds, and angels' too—
What words can say why Nature moves,
Why cells begin and planets die?

And even if revelation spoke in flame
From the sanctum in the far deep,
It wouldn't use our human tongue
But would hold up our hearts like a mirror to the sun—
And we would shine in the language of shining.

Something is stirring, outside speech.
I hear an orchestra rattle like tinnitus—
A sudden sun blasts me with silence—
And I know that shining is a language,
Shining is Nature's most sacred song.

## Home Comforts

Vodka shuts me off like a switch,
takes me back: a croquet lawn at night,
empty pavilion, silent shrubs—
looking in at party windows bright as gold
bass thumps insistent as a bully's tease....
How warm it must feel, the light of a soft woman.

All I hear is the thump of the drummer man—
drummer who drummed my child fevers,
drummed the fear into me like nails.

Tonight I admire the vodka's electricity;
sense each inch of home blindfold—
trail in the death hours of night the prints
of my finger-ends slowly
along the wall's fences and hillocks,
over the pyramid switch:
breathless, twist a wrist and open

to the smell of your warmth,
sizzling fresh as a farmhouse breakfast:
I nuzzle beside you, dive into dreams
where the drummer is silenced by your sighs;
where, crowned by suns, we bask
in our wild and tended garden,
scatter light like seeds.

# Dragon Song

Pinnochio has a nose,
But I've an honest tail:
With every breath of truth
I grow an extra scale.

People call me reptile
When they see my glistening scales,
But then I breathe from my heart;
It never, ever fails—

A blowtorch of flame
Comes flooding through my lips:
But then everyone starts to think
Of caves and chains and whips.

St. George! St. George, you coward!
You told the world a lie.
You forgot to tell the English
That I can never die.

So what, I loved a maiden—
But she loved me—
She loved my cave of secrets
And the underground sea.

St. George, St. George, we begged you
To come into the cave—
We would have shown you all the secrets
And the power that you crave.

But you sharpened up your lance
And you drove it through my heart;
You thought it was all over,
But that was just the start

Because I met her on the firebridge,
So radiant and so wise—
You couldn't make her happy,
So you cut her down to size.

But can you see her dancing now
From your ordered fields below?
She's the brightest in the East
With her songs like falling snow.

Through the dark I follow her,
I am her blazing tail.
I follow her silent music
On the very highest scale—

And if you listen in the night
In your deepest, darkest hour
You'll hear her whispers ringing
In the old bell tower

And then you'll hear her in the street
And you'll hear her in the trees
And you'll hear her in the tug of sails
On high English seas

And you'll hear her in a friend
And you'll hear her in my cry—
St. George, I have to tell you
That your dragon cannot die.

I am the wings inside you
I'm the tongue within the fire
And the thermals of my breath
Will always take you higher

Because, with her, I blaze the firebridge
To the source of everything—
I am the firebridge in your heart.
I'm the song that you will sing.

## Horse Whispering in the MIC

We got divorced from the horse, so now we're the cart leading — everything's fine Doctor, apart from this strange wooden feeling. . . . Did I ever suggest that the best method's breathing? But we're underwater with the sharks, gobbling blood in the harbour dark and with all these bitemarks in the wood, we could be sinking the ark! Try thinking pink like a flamingo, you won't sink when you let your wings go, and you won't wink as you whisper all you know; because *everything* flows. So wonder and wander as you would in the weird wild wood where the owl's howling like a wolf and there's a cleft in your hoof and Peter Pan is breathing fire like the dragon of truth; but if they can't stop the flames, they'll slice his head off as proof!

*They bring out the least in us to bring out the beast in us*
*They use their minds on us to blind us to the heart of us*

Everyone got drowned in the Big Brother pool — soon they'll be saying snuff movies aren't cruel — all empires are fuelled by divide and rule. Hide your big side or they'll find it and use it against you: they enter placentas to feed all the children an excessive percentage of longing and hatred! But when we play trains in the attic, the big sky is static, and Daddy's less manic, remembering his childhood and the fur in his hood: the kingdom never leaves you, it's easier to be true: look what just flew in, pixel by pixel, this fine flaming phoenix should easily fix this; but they say that landing is tricky when there's no aerodrome; the meaning gets mixed up on military phones

*They bring out the least in us to bring out the beast in us*
*They use their minds on us to blind us to the heart of us*

Now the winged horse is landing, standing on our screen:
why the military parade then, and the loaded magazines?
The big idea has always been fear; pedal that and we'll get
you all the gear: we'll get you the polar bear coats and some
coke in your goatee for some suicide boats and the votes of
the bloated; because they'll make you *long* for a piece of it—
start a little war, sell more arms, offer you the golden fleece
for it: the more we buy for buying's sake, the harder we
squeeze the trigger of our piece for it: the barrel of the gun
rests on the temple of love for it. . . . Take off your glove,
you're not an assassin! When they're asking you why, will
you say it was the gun that squeezed you? While the sun is
still free, take a ride on the wild horse in you

*Then you'll harvest the feast in us and the rising like yeast in us*
*As we're turning the mind of us to ride back to the heart of us*

# A Passer-By Demands Another Miracle
*for Suzanne Conway*

As if a ruby was a dancing-girl.
As if the wind was a flatterer's breath.
As if a seagull's eyes were made of pearl.
As if sleep was a measure of death.

As if the moon would shine without the sun.
As if my heartbeat in the manger knew.
As if this crown was easily won.
As if the many do not forget the few.

As if I'd torched the eyes inside his soul,
Stolen away his comfortable life.
As if his throat was not miracle enough,
His heart not drumming its own belief.

As if the sum was greater than the whole;
As if the whole story could ever be told.

# Page & Stage

How do you scan your fingers?
And what do you mean by those eyes?
I missed the bit you said just now.
I detest this constant surprise!

Please write it down on some paper
Then type it up nice and neat
Then send it off to be published
And *then* I can hear the beat

and the breath and the death of the wings by the nail that sings like a jackboot: Judas, you thought you'd sort it with your dosh and pulling strings, playing it rough, but we are such stuff as schemes like yours fade upon like butter in the burning wok; Dr Spock would've been proud of you, but the spirit growled at you, and you strung yourself up for the barking in your head: there's no larking with the dead, but if Judas sang on the melody of the resurrection boomerang, you'd hear behind the hell-fear the heaven-clear *if only: if only I'd heard then the breath of a monarch's wing, the sing my studies never heard, the world of the pearl thing:* welcome to the lightning of fire and ice, splicing beatitude into the attitude of the platitude, the blessing before the bang, stressing not where the ego-money's taken us, but the might of who we might be if your heart has not forsaken us; and are we so mistaken, we who love with our fingers and love with our eyes, who prize the surprise of the breath and the power greater than death that *cannot* be nailed down?

# Fire

> *The heart is nothing but a sea of fire*
> — Rumi

Hypnosis dances your eyes
back to the beginning.
The lone candle flares
its last golden message:
*There is a love
that burns us into love.*

Fire changes everything.
The darkness cowers, breathes
its last ashen breath,
for we can suspend fire
like suns for more lives
than we can think of.

The stars shine into your heart:
they never let you forget
that you burn to be like them.
Though darkness must come again,
when your doubt is deep enough,
all the suns will pour back in.

Hands will not blister
when they touch you, but long to be
the supernova you have become,
in your eyes, your slow grace:
you walked through hell: all are
aghast at your unburned lips;

the lips of a child that breathed
whatever was, and the world became.
In the swift hands of the wind,
or the curled palm of the waves,

the world became, and the child in you
stood naked by the shore.

You walked through the deep burning
gardens, singing of the Age Of Fire, listening
to the fire that roars now in your soul.
Everything is there; or here between the syllables,
beyond the whispers of meaning;
a new love burning in the silence.

## Bwindi Impenetrable National Park

Bwindi. Bwindi.
It means 'the place of darkness'.
An impenetrable forest of night,
The black hole at the core
Of the heart of darkness.
Bwindi. Bwindi.

Sun turns on the white mist
In the forest mountain dawn.
Silent walkers stride purposefully
Along a rare path—path
Of a thousand machetes,
A path with a heart, to the heart—
To the eyes of the silverback
And the simple secret of ourselves.

Moss has settled on the dangling
Parabola of a vine—
Green settles down with green—
The world is a root and a trunk
And we listen to the sap beating
To the rhythm of the morning.

It's a hard climb to the gorillas' nest,
To the thrones of green.
Here the tribe sat last night
In the thundering darkness,
Lashed by the fury of the drops,
Stiller than we can imagine—
As we sat restless and dumb,
Fidgeting with knives and forks,
As the gods nailed down
Our corrugated roof
In a frenzy of irritated drums—
And so the silence here

Of empty thrones
Seems still more silent,
Looking down
On the green crown of the valley.

The silverback would have sat here,
Above his tribe—
On the green throne carved by his weight,
Breathing his kingdom slowly.
Beside him, untouched,
So close to the might of his black palm,
Two butterfly-shaped pink blooms
Loop upwards on their stems
Like shaving mirrors.

Untouched.

Breathless, we follow the fresh path
To the rustlings and the grunts—
We know they are there, we know—
Then a patch of dark—a sudden star—
An eye!—and she is there,
Her baby on her back—
And he is there—a giant skull
And the world's most arrogant eyes,
Set deep in his mind—
The philosopher-king is there,
And now he is stripping the bark—
Bending the branches to him,
Bending his kingdom to his lips.

For an hour we thrill to
The Zen mastery of each gesture—
The effortless music of farting,
The arrogance of innocence:
The baby at play, learning

To bend the branches.

Their ways have made men listen:
They have been granted a kingdom.

In the foothills of these mountains
Enemies who slice machetes
Into the faces of women and children
Agreed on only this:
The mountain gorilla must be saved.

And then we leave them to their peace,
Suddenly aware of the machetes
That carved this path,
The power of a sharpened blade.

But the midday sun has lit up
Another tribe—the butterflies . . .

They dance around us like our hopes
And settle in clusters to eat,
Sucking the goodness from the stones.

We walk slower now, with still more reverent care
As everywhere the butterflies dance like confetti
Around us, they dance like praise around us.

So this is Bwindi. This is the place of darkness.
I ask our guide the local name for light.
'Omushana', he says.

*Bwindi Omushana*
*Bwindi Omushana*

*Omushana*

# Walk Out

Walk out of the house of time.
Walk through the paper screen of space.
Behind the party lights of stars
The fire burns without a face.

Though it is far, it is near.
It will melt your iron mind.
Much mightier than you dreamed,
But not impossible to find.

Watch your paper words in fire
How they incinerate to gold:
You are burning all your books
In the tale that can't be told.

Only then will you breathe again
In the music of the fire
And the golden dance will take you up
To the last ecstatic choir

And your wings in bliss will stretch
And the song of songs unfold
A symphony of blossoming
The libretto of the rose

And the cells ignite like stars
And the love like light is spread
Across the lightning circuits
Of the living and the dead

And now the walls have fallen down
And the paper's turned to dust:
The winds are free to take you,
And you must follow. You must.

## Sunday Morning

The things that go without saying—
The nothing-to-heal epiphanies of mornings
At home that leave the busy mind silent:
She's having a mad half hour to Kate Bush,
Our little boy in her arms, and he's laughing
Like the first time laughter broke the sky,
Giggling a rapture we never taught him
Because he's still dripping silver
From the first sacred stream—

He's not solemn or mannered or trying too hard.
My little boy is just giggling in his mother's arms:
And now they're face to face, cheeks on the floor,
And she's crying to *Moments Of Pleasure*
And he points at her tears and exclaims
With all the freshness of a toddler rolling
His tongue around the juice of a new word:
WET! And she cries a little more,
For the things that are left without saying.

# Eastbourne Cliffs
*for Laurence*

*Further, further, Daddy*

My little boy takes me further in the sun
Into a miracle where the white pebble
Sits in the chapel of a spring
By the white, white cliffs

And the trickle of the water
Is a rhythm of love:
It is love calling,
This water falling:

*Further, further, Daddy*

This water falling
On the white pebble
I place now in the secret box
I carry with me forever

For this is the same
White pebble
My son places
On my grave

*Further, further, Daddy*

And I can hear him clear
As a spring in the white cliff
From the far place
Where I cannot touch him

But where our listening,
Despite all the deep divides,
Splashes us together in the great light
In an everlasting wave of love.

# If Everyone Did

Let's have a scrap, let's do a rap—
Or scratch the silence—
A hip, a hip, a hip, a hip hop!

But hey now, whoa, I gotta stop,
'Cos I'm white, this ain't right—
An' I don't say *ain't*—it's too *quaint*—

I gotta apply some *fresh* paint
To this great rhythm poetry,
To this great rhythm poetry!

Now let's see; there's you out here,
And here's me—what about we shake
Some *juicy* fruit from the *universal* tree?

Put away that accent boy, be yourself—
Talk about brotherhood in your own voice!
But to be honest, if I had the choice,

I'd be a Jamaican-born Welshman—
*Reggae lovebeat ya bloodclot rastafari*
*Froma Nanny Town outsida wicked Kingston*

*Where da King is from*—Bob Marley, I am not so
Much worthy as to gather up the crumbs from under
Your table—but when I am able to integrate

Your redemption-fire with the higher
Purposes of the Welsh dragon-bards
*Singing like Sunday bells*

*Down the long valleys of the shadow*
*Of death that haunts us all, wherever*
*We are from*—I will sing my song:

Sing a song of England, what will you buy?
A Merc, a flat and Sky TV,
And don't ask why—

Entertain ourselves to death, forget who we are;
Cometic surgery is nice,
It won't leave a scar!

If you do not consume, you are *nothing!*
I consume air, turning to poison.
I consume water, turning to poison.

I consume the fruits of the earth
Genetically engineered by men
Whose wonder and piety have been *castrated!*

When I see the companies who want to patent genes . . .
When I see the men who sell addiction to the poor . . .
When I see the soldiers who bayonet the monks . . .

When I see the black fingernails of the man
With no family . . . when I see what I see
*Through the mirror* I consume fire like a fire-eater

I beat fire like a fire-beater—
I'm streetwise as a runaway
Cheetah in Camden Town!

But who needs the wisdom of the cynical street
When we know the wisdom of the beat
Beyond beyond and further beyond than that?

Which street are you wise on, anyhow?
Compton, Railton, Piccadilly, Camberwell?
EC1? N17? SE1? *All depends on your area, right?*

Let's walk together the universal street,
The beat of brotherhood above neighbourhood,
The beat of the blood in every heart

That says we've got to start being *ourselves*
Before everything else—yeah, but who the hell *are* we?
We, me; that's a little poem by Muhammad Ali; we, me . . .

My name is, my name is . . .
My name is Philip Wells
And I'm English and I'm a man—

*You're not a man, you're a soul*
*Struggling to weave together*
*The oppositional dualities*

*Of masculine and feminine, to become*
*Whole, to be full of radiant power,*
*To pass on the knowledge of the light . . .*

*And your name, Philip Wells; what was your*
*Original name before your grandparents were born?*
I am English—*Go back, go back*

I'm French, I'm a Viking—*Go back, go back*
I'm a caveman—*Go back, go back*
I'm a whale, an aphid, a stone! *Go back to the centre!*

*Where is your home star? Do you know, can you remember?*
*Have you ever listened to the cosmic hiss?*
*Ask your neighbours to please turn the noise down . . .*

*Turn the dimmer switch down on the streetglow*
*And there you have it—as many stars as all*
*The living things that have ever died . . .*

Northern lights brighter than fireworks . . .
A meteor crashes and burns in a comet-flash . . .
*What's that?* Oh, that's a Sky TV satellite—

*Does that tell us who we are too?*
Ladies and Gentlemen, ignore all previous pronouncements!
There will be endless celebrity-football-reality-makeovers

To amuse and *anaesthetise* you: there will be endless scenes
Of violence to make you appreciate just how lucky you are
That you're not being beaten to pulp right now!

We will try to avoid all *loving* sex wherever possible—
All *violent* sex gives everyone the important impression
That the sexes are perpetually at war which keeps everyone

*Apart* and *angry* and *hungry* for those (expensive)
*Compensatory* fixes: for all these (conveniently elusive)
Desires we have smaller buttons, bigger buttons,

Smaller screens, bigger screens, screens on every
Surface, Madam: direct debit? That'll do nicely.
Invest in cigarettes, one billion Chinese

Won't kick that habit: keep it all ticking along,
Ticketipoo: the computer Network won't crash—
Mother Nature can take it, technology'll solve it—

No such thing as a free meal, lad—
If everyone did that the whole friggin' place
Would grind to a halt—bloody do-gooder!

*If everyone did who everyone was* . . .
We don't have words for that kind of joy.
Identity is the bridge we cross from emptiness to wholeness—

When we reach the light on the other side, we no longer need
That bridge, though we praise and praise the wisdom
Of the genius who built that bridge—

*If everyone did who everyone was—*
I know it and I've seen it, I live it and I say it—
If everyone did who everyone was

Mother Earth would wake up, remember who she was—
And the whole world would change from the inside out
And your beautiful grandchild will be teaching you,

By firelight to the sound of the waves under the stars,
All the knowledge of the light—and you'll remember it all. . . .
And fear will dissolve in the blaze of the sun, and new rains

Will come; new hearts will bloom and fight with courage
Against the fearful and the cynical, so new hearts will be free
To bloom again—and all because, once, one person

Listened truly to another who said
*If everyone did who everyone was—*
And because, soon, *everyone* began to listen . . .

And because now, everyone does who everyone *is*—
And it's *better than heaven*—just because now,
Everyone *does* who everyone *is.*